Waiting on the Last Train

Waiting on the Last Train

Poems by

Terry Allen

© 2022 Terry Allen. All rights reserved.
This material may not be reproduced in any form, published,
reprinted, recorded, performed, broadcast,
rewritten or redistributed without
the explicit permission of Terry Allen.
All such actions are strictly prohibited by law.

Cover design by Shay Culligan

ISBN: 978-1-63980-136-7

Kelsay Books
502 South 1040 East, A-119
American Fork, Utah 84003
Kelsaybooks.com

for Nancy

Acknowledgments

The author is grateful to the editors of the following journals, where these poems first appeared, some in earlier versions:

Black Fox Literary Review: "Them"

Boundless Anthology: "Save the Marmots!"

Constellations: "Woodpeckers"

Down in the Dirt: "Skeletor Learned a Valuable Lesson," "Primordial Ghosts"

I-70 Review: "Our Lady of the Angels"

Interpretations: "Physics and Poetry Entwine in the Multiverse"

The Madison Review: "Capricorn"

Modern Poetry Quarterly Review: "Tornado"

Third Wednesday: "Larry," "The Things They Left Behind"

Well Versed: "Drifting Away," "Defying the Law of Gravity," "Free Pain Evaluation for You or Your Horse," "Follow Your Bliss," "Annabelle and Barney"

Contents

Primordial Ghosts	13
Drifting Away	14
The Things They Left Behind	16
Them	17
Annabelle and Barney	19
Waiting on the Last Train	20
Kay Matheson Dead at Age Eighty-Four	22
Free Pain Evaluation for You or Your Horse	23
Two Old Friends Talk of Jenny While Flaneuring on a Summer Afternoon	24
Baileys Spiked Coffee	28
Freshman English	30
Capricorn	31
The Will to Live	32
Save the Marmots!	35
The Spear Carriers	37
The Test	40
Tornado	41
The Studio Era on Poverty Row	42
Defying the Law of Gravity	44
Physics and Poetry Entwine in the Multiverse	46
Sarah Bernhardt	47
Let the Games Begin	49
Two Barflies Talk Politics and Trucks Over Bourbon and Beer	53
Thoughts on an Odd State of Affairs	55
Our Lady of the Angels	57
Woodpeckers	58
In the End All Things Will Be Known, but No One Will Be There to Know Them	60
Clara Blandick and The Great Adventure	61

Larry	62
Follow Your Bliss	64
Skeletor Learned a Valuable Lesson This Week	66
On the Bookshelf at Night	67

"I'm well dressed, waiting on the last train."
Bob Dylan, *Things Have Changed*

Primordial Ghosts

A sprinkling of cosmic dust
from the edge of creation
gathers in the dark corner
of the bookshelf
next to Raymond Chandler's
The Long Goodbye.

Drifting Away

at the crest of the hill
under the quarter moon
dimmed by falling snow

silhouetted by one
haloed streetlamp
winter has been busy

the street is banked and white
a gust of wind picks up
and fresh flakes swirl about them
as if they are fixed
frozen forever
in a Christmas snow globe

years pass
the couple marries
memories fade

he visits her now
in a home that's not theirs
where her mind sometimes drifts

to a winter night
when the Lady of Time
brought the purest

white flying carpet
that took them for a ride
into their prosaic lives

The Things They Left Behind

Have you heard anything about Lon Chaney? my wife asks. And in the split second before I answer, pictures of Lon Chaney come to my mind and I realized that I am thinking immediately of Lon Chaney, Jr. and not his father, who famously starred in the silent film version of *The Phantom of the Opera* in the 1920s, and I'm not sure which one she is asking me about, but really it's Junior who has made the biggest impression on me and I can clearly see him as if he's still with us as Lenny talking to George about the rabbits in *Of Mice and Men* and as the retired sheriff with the crippled, arthritic hands in *High Noon* who tells Will Kane that he can't help him because he can't even hold a gun anymore and Will would only be worrying about him if there is any trouble, and then, of course, I see Lon Chaney as *The Wolf Man,* a role that changed his acting career forever. And I also think of Tim O'Brien, who wrote the collection of Vietnam War stories, *The Things They Carried,* and I say to myself, yes, that's right. That's true, but it's also the things they left behind, like these wonderful characters. And being a little confused at this point, I ask my wife to repeat what she asked me. *What?* I say. *Have you heard anything about Liz Cheney?* she asks again. *No,* I reply.

Them

They say that evil can only thrive in darkness, at least that's what the wealthy politician said in a speech at the Holocaust Memorial Museum National Day of Remembrance, but then again, he didn't know much about history and really only read the speech written by someone else, each word fashioned from dry brittle leaves, crumbling as he spoke. But perhaps the idea of evil thriving in darkness may have been what your doctor had in mind when he asked you if you only saw them at night, and you said yes, it was after midnight when the man in the western plaid snap shirt appeared in the shadows, reflected in the bedroom mirror, and you told the doctor how you yelled at the man to get out, but he just stood still staring at you, and it was then you turned on the light and ran to get a hammer to protect yourself and ended up searching the house, because you couldn't find him and then remembered to check the doors to see how he got in, but you found they were locked and that's when the doctor told you they don't like the light and advised you to use nightlights, which you did until several months later when you thought they were gone, and you unplugged the nightlights and that's when you rolled over in bed and saw the old woman with vacant sunken eyes peering at you from beneath the sheets. After that you not only used the nightlights again, you told the doctor, but you also kept a flashlight close by at all times. *That's good,* the doctor said. *That should keep them away.* You thought so, too, you told the doctor. You really did, until you read a sad story about how a young woman preparing to become a nun was raped and murdered in broad daylight four decades ago in West Virginia and no one was ever caught and punished for her death and then later you watched a program on the History Channel about Vlad the Impaler who sadistically killed as many as 100,000 people, most of them in the cold light of day and the next afternoon you were in your sun room and looked up to see two women with no feet floating toward you, who kept repeating that it was time for you to go and tried to put a handkerchief over your face. *Oh my,* the doctor said, and you replied that was when you remembered it was mid-morning when the politician spoke at the Holocaust Museum, and now you can't sleep at all.

Annabelle and Barney

All right, here's another one. This is of our dog Barney, who was a mix with a whole lot of hound in him. He was a pooch who liked to chase rabbits and squirrels and had loads of love to give. A big-hearted old boy. And this is a photo of our daughter Annabelle, who was named after her great-grandmother. Anyway, this picture was taken around the time she graduated from high school. As you can see, it was a staged photo that she planned all by herself. It was taken on a country road outside of town, around noon on a spring day, 'cause she wanted the sunlight and the shadows just right. Some people think she's walking toward our home, but we lived in town next to the hardware store that was started by my grandfather and his brother. Anyway, Anna was not only interested in the light and dark in the photo, but she had a lot to say about the meaning of the road and fences and trees, and the colors of everything, especially the yellow line which she said was a symbol of optimism, joy, creativity, and the presence of God. All that's true, I guess, but as the years have passed, and I look at the photo now, all I can see is the vanishing point in the distance that she's walking toward.

Waiting on the Last Train

An elderly couple dances in each other's arms. He sings softly.

I'm the Sheik of Araby. Your love belongs to me.
What made you think of that?
It was used twice in the score of Fellini's *8 ½*.

Was it? I don't recall.
At night when you're asleep, into your tent I'll creep.
That sounds creepy, all right.
It was written in 1921.
Before my time.
It's in the public domain now and has become a jazz standard.
    Maybe I should record it.
In your dreams.
Aye, there's the rub.

Never mind your musical fantasies. How are you doing?
Most of my parts are working, I think.
That's good. How are your hips?
I like my right one better than my left.
You're still having pain?
A bit.

Do you think Guido killed himself in the end of the movie?
Possibly. Do you?
Well, he did crawl under the table and shoot himself in the head.
True. But he also escapes a traffic jam in the beginning of the film
    by climbing out of the vehicle's window and floating over rows
    of cars and ascending into the clouds.
That's Fellini's fantasy of escaping a stifling situation.

Maybe crawling under a table and shooting himself is another
    fantasy about escape.
Maybe. But I like the ambiguity.

The stars that shine above, will light our way to love.
If you can't correct the problem, incorporate it, I guess.
You'll roam this land with me.
I know. *You're the Sheik of Araby.*
To the very end.
To the end.

Kay Matheson Dead at Age Eighty-Four

For the last twenty years of her life, Kay Matheson lived in a nursing home in the Northwest Highlands with her beloved dog (alas, the pup's name is unknown at this time) where Kay would tell of the Christmas Day in 1950 when she and three companions "retrieved" the Stone of Scone from Westminster Abbey and brought it back to Scotland. *I have no regrets,* she would say, *apart from losing my toes, when the block of red sandstone dropped on my foot, but I'm managing fine without them.* Her dog, though elderly and not missing any parts, is doing fine, as well, but needs a new home.

Free Pain Evaluation for You or Your Horse

Sign painted on a trailer in Columbia, Missouri

Have you ever had your horse travel
freely in a circle to the right,
but fight you tooth and nail
when you ask for the other direction?

Does your horse have a contracted heel
on one foot that won't get any better
despite the best efforts
of your hoof-care professional?

Have you or your horse been battling
performance or lameness issues
and don't know what to do next
except to flare your nostrils, hang your head,
and walk slowly to the right?

I'll be down the road from your place,
Thursday next,
and can stop by to take a look-see.

I can't perform miracles,
but I'll do the best I can
for the horse.

Two Old Friends Talk of Jenny While Flaneuring on a Summer Afternoon

Do you know what these yellow flowers are called?
Opposite-Leaved Golden Saxifrage, I think.
You might be on to something...
I thought as much.
If...
Yes?
If we were walking about in Europe beside a shady stream, but...
But?
In this case, we're looking at Creeping Jenny.
Really?
Oh, yes.
They're quite attractive.

Here's a quiz for you.
I do like a good quiz.
Are you ready?
I am.
Who was it that said, *Jenny is the most beautiful name in the wide world?*
Winston Churchill.
Winston Churchill?
Yes.
Where did you come up with that?
Winston's mother.
His mother?
Her name was Jennie Jerome.
Was it?
It was.

Well, I'm afraid there's no prize this time.
What do you mean?
The answer to the quiz is Forrest Gump.
He said that?
He did.
Well, isn't that remarkable. It is a nice name.

Did you know that Jenny in Irish is S-e-a-n-n-a-f-a-i-r?
If you say so.
Pronounced as Shan-a-fur.
That's nice.
And Jenny in Welch is S-i-a-n-i.
Is it?
Pronounced Shah-nee.
Oh, my.

And Jenny in Scottish…
That's remarkable you should mention Scottish. It makes me think.
About what?
Winston Churchill was an adopted Scot, according to his family.
We may be steering a bit off course now.
Did you know he commanded the Royal Scots Fusiliers during the Great War?
Well, did you know that in the original novel, Forrest Gump flies into space?
Really?
With a male orangutan called Sue.
Sue?
That's right.

I like Jenny better.
It is a lovely name.
It is to me.
Yes. I see that.

Jenny died, didn't she?
She did in the movie, I'm afraid.
That's sad.
In the novel she marries an assistant sales manager for a roofing business.

I was once married, you know.
Were you?
A long time ago really.
In the distant past.
We were quite young at the time.
Weren't we all?
She was very fond of flowers…like these.

You never get over these things.
You don't.

Put one foot in front of the other. That's all we can do.
That's right.

Off we go then.
You lead. I'll saunter behind.
Saunter?

I've been wanting to use that word for a long time now.
Well, why not.
We only live once.

Baileys Spiked Coffee

The old gentleman sits by himself
in the dimmed light
at his favorite corner table in the jazz club,
keeping warm on a bitter cold winter night,
and listening to the quartet play,
All the Things You Are.

And that's just fine by him.
It's a sensuous and tender song
that he liked to play on the piano
when his arthritic hands didn't betray his efforts
to bring to life Jerome Kern's lovely melody.

It's this piece that reminds him of his wife
who passed away two or three years ago.
Although, now, he's not entirely certain.
Often, he can't recall how long he's been alone
and that's when, he feels her presence,
and he thinks she may not have left at all,
but may be waiting for him somewhere
in the deep shadows of their home,
It's in these fleeting moments
that he hears her voice
and finds himself speaking out loud to her,
often about small things, like the weather
or the late mail delivery on a rainy afternoon.

And now, in the last year or so, he sees her
for just a moment. Usually it's late at night,
sometimes she's sitting in a chair,
silhouetted by the picture window,
looking at him from across the room,
or she's passing by the bedroom door.

I should talk to someone about this,
he finds himself saying aloud
as the quartet takes the lush music
for an improvised turn around the room.

*I'll make an appointment next week
and talk to the doctor,* he thinks
as he sips the last of his drink
and sits back and is carried away
to a time when the air was warm
and his wife was near,
just as she is now, sitting close to him,
her eyes closed, listening to the music,
and keeping time with her translucent hand
on the table near his.

Freshman English

I recall the first college class I attended was an English course and our first assignment was to listen as the instructor read a passage aloud and to write out exactly what he was reading with all the correct spelling, punctuation and grammar required. *Thank god for Mrs. Shields, my senior-high school, college-prep, English teacher,* I thought. *I can do this;* however, it turned out that the passage he read mostly contained dialogue, and it also turned out that he stammered and repeated himself, but I wrote out exactly what he was saying, repetitions of sounds, words and phrases included because I wasn't sure if it was part of the dialogue or not. Of course, I knew later that he had a speech problem, but the saddest part of that memory was thinking about when he was fired three years later after it was discovered that he had lied on his application. He not only had no advanced degrees at all, but he had written his own letters of recommendations and forged all his documents, but he showed he must have had some writing ability and that's how he ended up teaching freshman English.

Capricorn

Right now, you may be feeling the weight of a Komodo dragon on your shoulders. But I want you to know that it's not as bad as you imagine. All righteous algorithms are in harmony as the planets align in your favor. Can you rise to that higher level to see the difference between a raven and an albatross? I believe you can. Know that you're not defined by your past like that time in college when you took a part-time job with the grounds crew over the Christmas break, and you only lasted half a day after you were assigned to make the rounds with one of the full-time employees in a beat-up maintenance truck, and it only took less than a minute once the doors were closed for you to be overwhelmed by the stench of dust, oil, and body odor mixed with the hot air of the truck's heater. And that's when your senior partner took out a crumpled metal Band-Aid box from his coat pocket that looked as if he had rescued it from a dump, and he pulled out a homemade cigarette and lit up inside the closed vehicle, chain-smoking all morning, and you tried not to breathe, but failed, although you were able to remain conscious, knowing that if you passed out, you were sure to succumb to smoke poisoning, but as is usual with your sign, you soldiered on no matter how daunting the tasks, taking one moment at a time and putting one foot in front of the other just as you will do this very day.

The Will to Live

At age ten my son said that he had a dream,
a fervent wish to survive until the end,
until the final curtain, until he could take his bow
with the rest of the cast, smiling at the audience,
as if to say, I made it. I came out alive in this one.

I understood what he was saying, but I hadn't thought
about what he was feeling until then. I could tell
he had been chewing on this for some time.

As a stage director, it's sometimes easier to cast
your own children in a play, easier to get them to
and from rehearsals, easier to deal with a stage
parent, particularly if you are that parent.

I cast him first in *The Grapes of Wrath*
at age seven, where he played the dead child
at the campsite of refugee farm families
on their way to California.

Then, at age eight, I cast him as MacDuff's son
in William Shakespeare's tragedy *Macbeth*.
The boy appears in only one scene, where he
banters with his mother and then is murdered
by Macbeth's thugs. At least in this play,
he had a chance to perform a character,
a cute and clever boy who just happens
to be stabbed to death by scene's end.

Two years later, at age ten, he was cast
as one of the children in *Ghetto,*
Joshua Sobol's play about the experiences
of the Jews of the Vilna Ghetto
during Nazi occupation in World War II.
This time he got to act and to sing and to dance,
since the play is about the theatre company
in the ghetto; however, after their final
performance and after singing *Ode to Joy*
in German, the SS commander in charge
guns them down with his submachine gun.

After that my son became obsessed
with Schopenhauer and the will to live,
something he picked up from the cast.
That's what happens when your son
is in a play with university students,
where at least one of them is taking
German courses and another is in
a philosophy class, where the phrase
wille zum leben is all the rage.

A few months later, still ten-years-old,
he got his wish when he bounded on stage
a wide grin on his face, bowing with such
bravado at the curtain call, as if he had played
the principal role in *The Taming of the Shrew,*
and for him, he had. This was a big deal.
This was a moment to celebrate.

As one of Petruchio's comic servants,
he had excelled at physical humor,
and he had survived through it all.

After that, he was heard saying aloud
to cast and crew, *Okay, what's next?*

Save the Marmots!

This is all I have. I'm sorry. I'd gladly give more if I had it.
We all do what we can.
It seems like a worthy cause…
Oh, it is.
Support the Save the Marmot Wildlife Fund!
Oh, yes.
I don't know much about it, really. It's hard to keep up on everything.
It is.
Although I do my best. I read a bit here and there, and I watch news programming now and then just to find out what's going on in the world. Marmots are foxlike animals, aren't they? Sort of like a short, wild dog sort of thing?
Let me help you. A marmot is a rather large ground squirrel, actually. There are fifteen species found in Asia, Europe and North America, if I'm not mistaken
No, you're quite right. I remember now. You've got your Alaska marmot and your Alpine marmot and your black-capped marmot from eastern Siberia.
With each donation of $20, we give you a t-shirt with a picture of a marmot riding a bicycle.
Are they circus animals?
Not in the least. Just try getting a Himalayan marmot to do acrobatics and sleight of hand and see what happens.
Perhaps the Vancouver Island marmot would be capable.
Well yes. The Vancouver Island marmot is another matter entirely.
But not the Himalayan marmot?

Oh, heaven's no.

Do you take checks?

Oh, yes, with proper identification, of course, and a $15 check service fee.

The Spear Carriers

They had not meet until the first read-through
for the winter production of *Macbeth,*
but they didn't really have a chance to speak.
In fact, neither one had lines in the play.
They were to be part of the crowd.
Walk-ons. Extras. Bit-Players. Supernumeraries.
In this production they were told by the director
that they would be known as spear carrier
number one and spear carrier number two
which meant that they were background people
who filled in a scene without saying anything,
or drawing undo attention to themselves.

They finally did have a chance to meet;
however, at the first rehearsal
when they waited offstage for their cue
to make their first entrance with King Duncan.

Hi, I'm Maureen.
Hi Maureen. I'm Sean.
I like your spear, Sean.
I know. I know. It's just a broom handle.
Yes, it is.
I grabbed it from home.
Are we supposed to use rehearsals props already?
I just wanted to make a good impression.
I get it. I guess.
This is my first big role.
Really?

I played a dead soldier in *Mother Courage* last year.
I saw that.
It wasn't easy.
I don't remember seeing you.
I did the best I could to bring the character to life.
I should have paid closer attention.

And, of course, that's when they missed their cue
and their first entrance; however, the scene
went on without them and when notes
were given at the end of the rehearsal,
they discovered that they were not missed.
And that's how it went from that moment on.
Their lot was to be there or not to be there,
but most importantly, they were to be players
in this great tragedy who in the end
were not to be missed. When the bodies
piled up, no member of the audience
was to ask another member of the audience,
what happened to the spear carriers?

But never you mind, the two actors,
Maureen and Sean, had become friends
through it all and could be seen spending
time together at the cast party,
toasting their success on stage and off,
paying little attention, at first,

to the loud shrieks of the weird sisters
who chased Macbeth around the sofa
with a bowl of guacamole dip,
chanting, *Something wicked this way comes!*

I'd like to have a line or two next time, said Maureen
That would be nice, said Sean
Something clever, said Maureen.
I'd like that, too, said Sean.
Or maybe just, "Good day, Sir," said Maureen.
Or, "How's your mum?" said Sean.
That way, we'd make an impression, said Maureen.
We would, said Sean.
And in the end, we'd be remembered, said Maureen.
We would, indeed, said Sean.

The Test

There's something about going to the eye doctor in anticipation of being able to see the world again, in focus with all its thorny details revealed in living color, although it doesn't help that you're color blind, at least the red-green kind, which might make some sense if you couldn't see red or green, but you do see red and green if the colors are deeply saturated and bold; however, when you're asked to take a color-blind test every single year by identifying the pattern revealed in each page of some special "color-blind identification book," and you can only see the pattern in page one and no more, that's when you ask if it's possible to have been miraculously cured of your color blindness since the last time you took the test? *No, that's not possible,* you're told by the young lady giving the test, as if she's explaining something to someone with dementia. And that's when she looks at you as if she's detected something that needs to be reported to higher authorities. But then later you're relieved when you see the results of your exam that reports that you seemed to know where you were, and you appeared to know why you were there, and that you *were* able to repeat the words cleverly sneaked in early in the exam: *banana, sunset,* and *chair.*

Tornado

1893

In the downpour and darkness,
it swept southeast for six miles,
cutting across the Kansas prairie,
leaving not a house, barn, tree,
or headstone standing in its path.

At the Hutchinson farm, seven horses
were killed and Mrs. Hutchinson
lost her life. Her arms and legs were found
in a treetop a mile away from where
she had prepared the evening meal
an hour before.

As soon as the storm had passed,
the awful hunt began. All night long,
with lanterns in hand, neighbors searched
for the dead and dying. The last body
was discovered the next afternoon.

And on a Sunday three days later,
the Union Pacific ran special trains
to Williamstown for sightseers
to view the damage.

The Studio Era on Poverty Row

The director on a movie set takes one of the actors aside.

Wayne, what's the problem?
I don't know. Just nerves, I think.
I'd tell you to relax and don't worry, but…
Thanks.
I'd tell you that, but we have sixty people standing around…
I know
Sixty people.
I know.
Cast and crew.
I'm sorry.
And really, Wayne, we have to get this scene in the can and move on.
I can do it.
Can you?
I know I can do it.
We've already done twenty-eight takes.
I know I've let you down, but I'm ready.
That's good, Wayne.
Thanks.
Because you know you've only got one line in the scene.
I know.
You run in when you hear Melinda say, "Roger, I want to confess."
You're right.
Run in as soon as the word *confess* is said.
It might help if I started sooner.
That's been part of the problem, Wayne. You can't step on her line.

No, of course, not.
She has to get it out, especially the word *confess*.
Understood.
Good.
I'm ready.
Good.
I'm focused.
Good. Now, the other thing is to make sure that you bring in the platter.
Platter?
Yes. The platter with the fish.
The fish. The fish. Right. Right. Oh, god! That's right!
Got it?
Yes. Run in with the platter.
And the fish. Don't forget the fish this time.
I won't. I'm feeling good about this now.
Let's try one more, Wayne.
Got it. I listen, and I run in with the platter and the fish.
And then you say?
Oh, god! I've gone blank. I can't remember…
Focus, Wayne and breathe.
It may be the smell that's throwing me off.
What smell, Wayne?
I think the fish is going bad. It's making me dizzy.
It's rubber, Wayne. It's not real. It's a rubber fish.
Oh, no! I'm going to be sick.

Defying the Law of Gravity

Friends up north ask, *So, what's it like there?* As they try to imagine someone giving up ice fishing and winter carnivals to move five hundred miles away into the heart of the Deep South, which I've always found peculiar and have sometimes suggested they might want to look at a map. *So, what's it like there?* they continue to ask. *All right, I say. This will give you an idea. There seems to be four major industries down here: education, health care, insurance, and...predatory lending.* That's when they usually smirk and ask if I'm joking. Like I would joke about signs at every major intersection advertising payday loans, title loans, cash advance loans, check into cash loans, rainy day loans, short-term mortgage loans, roll-over loans and no credit–we don't care loans. *Really? Does that make sense?* I'm asked. That's when I remind them that it doesn't have to make sense, after all it was Bugs Bunny who said, *I know this defies the law of gravity, but I never studied law!* And I tell them about driving past the university sports stadium in town and hearing screaming voices chant, *We're Number One! We're Number One!* And I don't know if they're cheering for their sports team or for the fact that the state *is* number one in predatory lending with rates of 400–1200% interest. *How could a state let that happen?* they ask. Well, I explain it probably has little to do with the millions of dollars the industry charitably donates to legislators who are only concerned with making loans available to citizens that are in desperate need. And that's when I tell them about a bill that is awaiting the governor's signature that will open up new, thinking-outside-the-box, possibilities for predatory loans. In fact, in anticipation of the bill's becoming law, three locations are already in place and advertising the grand opening for "Big Bob's You Got 'Em. We get 'Em Body Tissue and Organ Loans."

Physics and Poetry Entwine in the Multiverse

All structures exist mathematically.
All possible worlds are real.

Planets can be spherical,
or triangular, or square, or pentagonal.
And they can be donut shape, too,
with a hole in the middle,
but for that to happen,
they have to be spinning so fast
they are on the verge
of breaking apart.

Still:

All possible worlds are real.

At the heart of philosopher Robert Nozick
principle of fecundity is the belief
that everything one imagines exists.

Can this be easily explained?
It doesn't matter.

After all, it was John Butler Yeats who said,
What can be explained is not poetry.

Sarah Bernhardt

I toured a *Mummies of the World* exhibit and walked away thinking of Sarah Bernhardt, a famous French stage actress who starred in some of the most popular plays of the late nineteen and early twentieth centuries, a remarkable woman who kept a satin-lined coffin in her bedroom and sometimes slept in it or lounged there to study her roles. She was called the queen of the pose and the princess of the gesture, the lady with the golden voice. She performed all over the world, made eight films and endorsed face cream, cars and real estate, sometimes accessorized with a dead bat and toured America with one of her many pet animals, an alligator named Ali-Gaga. Still, Sarah liked to sleep in a coffin, and she liked to tell people she liked to sleep in a coffin, and she liked to pose in her coffin for photographs, adding to the legend she created about herself. She was truly a woman who for sixty years pioneered the cult of celebrity, but the public can be fickle and fame is fleeting and so when she died in Paris on a Monday, March 26, 1923, something was already brewing, something momentous had occurred just four months earlier, two thousand miles away in Egypt's Valley of the Kings, that would shake the very pedestal her coffin rested on when two archaeologists became the first living souls in more than three thousand years to enter King Tutankhamen's tomb and find that his sealed burial chamber was intact as was the stone sarcophagus that contained three coffins nested within each other. Inside the final coffin, made of solid gold, was the mummified body of the boy-king. Eighty-five years later, Sarah was still resting peacefully out of the limelight when King Tut's remains were transferred to a high-tech glass display case, whereupon TV camera crews, photographers, and journalists descended like a plague of locusts, creating an atmosphere fit for a modern-day movie star.

Let the Games Begin

I began to settle in
as a new faculty member
at a Midwestern university
when I decided to change
my office arrangement
by moving the desk
from one wall to another,
which I mentioned
to two new colleagues
at lunch as their eyes
widened, and a deep disquiet
filled their faces.

They said be very careful,
don't touch anything and
call the "movers office"
to do the job for me. I asked
if I couldn't just stop by
the office, and they said
no one knows where
it's located.

All right, I said.

Still, be forewarned, one
colleague told me.
*When they arrive, don't
speak unless spoken to*

*first, don't make direct
eye contact and above all
never point at anything.*

And if you do gesture,
the other colleague said,
*do it slowly and make
sure both of your hands
are completely visible
at all times.*

*I'm getting a little nervous
about this,* I said.

No! they said. *Never show
that you're nervous,
and never let them smell fear.*

That was that and when
the arrangement was made
and the movers arrived,
two beefy men came into
the office to do the job,
while a third somber figure
stood outside to watch
and supervise the work.

When they left, and I felt
safe to move out of the corner,

I rolled my desk chair into position
and that's when the phone
rang. I picked up and listened
to yet another supervisor on the line.

She wanted to know if the workers
had moved the desk and if indeed
they were supervised
by a supervisor.

Yes, I said.

You didn't move anything yourself?

Oh, no.

*I'm sending someone over there
now to take your statement.
Just tell us in your own words
exactly what happened.*

I will, I said, and I hung up
and began to panic, knowing
that I had moved the chair.

And for the rest of that year
I felt I was being closely
watched, and I could hear odd
clicking noises when I
used my office phone.

It also didn't help
when my department chair
told me that one of the members
of the music faculty
had mysteriously disappeared
a couple of years back.
It seemed that a choir
was about to perform
at an outdoor concert
on campus when a rainstorm
came up, and she had moved
a riser.

Two Barflies Talk Politics and Trucks Over Bourbon and Beer

He's at it again.
Who?
Senator Bonehead.
What's he done now?
He's spewing revisionist history like a cone geyser in Yellowstone Park.
As if we're too dimwitted to know better.
Our party never did this. Our party never did that.
Gaslighting 101 is what it is.
We never tried to rig the system.
Oh, yeah?
We'd all be better off if he revised the history of the Visigoths instead.
That'd keep him busy.
You know he'd be blowing smoke about the Visigoths sacking Rome in the fourth century B.C.
What a laugh. Pull the other one. It's got brass bells on it.
You know that and I know that.
It wasn't the Visigoths that sacked Rome on July 18, 387 B.C.
It was the Gallic Celts.
Led by the warlord Brennus, if I recall correctly.
Right you are.
I've always been good with warlord trivia.
You know that July 18 is considered a cursed day in Rome even now.
Really? I was unaware.
I recall that factoid because July 18 is when I met my first wife.

There's a coincidence for you.
The Visigoths didn't sack Rome until the fifth century B.C.
After they'd journeyed quite some distance across the Rhine and the Danube, I believe.
But our senator would have us believe they were just stopping by Rome for a hot bath.
I don't know how he got elected anyway.
The voters were scraping the bottom of the septic tank with that one.
Wait…wait a minute.
What?
Would you look at that?
Where?
Across the street. By the bank.
Wow!
You can say that again…front ways and back.
Nice Truck!
Oh, yeah!

Thoughts on an Odd State of Affairs

It may be that the times have changed everywhere, but all I know is that this never happened in the thirty years when I was living in the great frozen north, but now that I'm here, it happens all the time. I make an appointment, say with the dentist or the eye doctor or with the dealership to get my car serviced, and I immediately get an email or text message or both reminding me of my appointment and then two weeks before the appointment, I again get a text message followed by an email reminding me of my appointment. These are then followed by phone calls reminding me that I have an appointment and if a voice mail is left, I'm instructed to call back and tell them I got the phone call and that I understand I have an appointment at a certain time on a certain date, and just imagine the intensity of reminders that happen the day before and the day of the appointment. And that might be the end of it, except that once the appointment is over, I get home and find a message that wants me to fill out a survey about my appointment. Now I know that the nickname of our adopted state is *The Show-Me State,* which one legend attributes to a U.S. Congressman who said in a speech at the close of the nineteenth century that *Frothy eloquence neither convinces nor satisfies me. I am from Missouri. You have got to show me.* Although, there's another version of the Show-Me legend that I take to have greater truth. It concerns a miners' strike in Colorado in the 1890s that brought in a number of miners from Missouri to take the place of the strikers. The Missouri miners weren't familiar with Colorado mining methods and required repeated instructions. Pit bosses began saying, *That man is from Missouri. You'll have to show him.* And one story goes that a pit boss called the Missouri miners over and said, *All right, now I need to show you boys something and I want you to follow along. You need to use two hands operating a shovel, one placed here and the other placed there. And then you bend over and scoop. Mind that you use your legs and not your back. All right, let's try it again.* So, maybe the folks around here just need a few more reminders or a few more instructions. In fact, my wife says we're actually living in *The Draw-Me-a-Picture State.*

Our Lady of the Angels

The seat of the fire
that would kill ninety-two
students and three nuns
was in the rear stairwell
at the northeast corner
of the "U"-constructed school.
The first fire truck raised
ladders and opened the roof.
The inferno had already reached
the second floor when
the firemen began dropping
children into life nets
on the sidewalk below.
The ceiling of the second-floor
corridor fell in and sent
a blast of super-heated air
and gases throughout
the school, snuffed out
every ounce of life of those
still caught in the building.
Still, the firefighters managed
to push the blaze back out
the roof with fog and then fight
their way to the north side
into the classrooms where
they found children still
seated at their desks,
Veterans with thirty years
experience had never
witnessed such a sight.

Woodpeckers

My wife is a list maker
and I'm not. It's a perfect
relationship, since she plans
for a trip to the grocery store
days in advance, and I
treat the whole experience
as improvisational theatre.

But then sometimes I find
her list on the kitchen counter
growing as we get closer
to the big day, and I can't help
but add to it every once
in a while just for our
amusement by writing
woodpecker on the list
between *fruit* and *milk*.

And later, when we're
at the store, and she's
systematically filling
the cart, and I'm wandering
aimlessly about, looking
for inspiration, I'm really
waiting for her to discover
my amazing creativity,
but when we're finally heading
for the checkout line,

and she hasn't said
anything, I ask if she
found everything on the list,
and that's when she says
that she did, and I act surprised
as I pick through the items
in the cart.

Are you sure? I ask.

And that's when she says,
Well, almost everything.
The woodpeckers
were picked over,
a little too squishy and gray,
and really past their
sell-by date.

She says this, of course,
over her shoulder as she
turns the cart into
the nearest checkout line
and makes a large check mark
in the air.

In the End All Things Will Be Known, but No One Will Be There to Know Them

It's just as well because if there is a quiz show,
there would be no host to welcome the viewing audience
when there is no audience and no contestants;
otherwise, it would be pretty dull because everyone
would know the answers as they are read
to eager participants and a bored audience in the studio
and at home who would shout the answers out loud
even before the questions were completely asked,
and I wouldn't even be there to point out
the depressing fact that there is a quiz show
on weekday mornings at ten a.m. being broadcast
from a studio that sits empty with no one to operate
the cameras or even turn on the lights or do a sound
check for a program sponsored by unnecessary pharma
or insurance companies that hope their ads
are so clever and funny that nonexistent consumers
would be persuaded to pay for only what they need
and to ask their doctors who aren't there anymore
if Bullshitza is right for them.

Clara Blandick and The Great Adventure

Best remembered for her role
as Auntie Em in the 1939 film classic,
The Wizard of Oz,
Clara had a career of fifty years,
often playing eccentric elderly matriarchs
on stage and on the silver screen,
starting in 1901 at age twenty-five
and continuing through 1950
when she retired from acting
as her health deteriorated
and her eyesight began to fail,
and she suffered from severe,
painful arthritis. Then on April 15, 1962,
at age eighty-five, she returned home
from Palm Sunday services
at her church and rearranged
her room by placing her favorite photos
and memorabilia in prominent places
and laid out her resume
with a collection of press clippings
from her long career. She dressed
herself in an elegant royal blue
dressing gown and with her hair
properly styled, she took an overdose
of sleeping pills and lay down on a couch,
covering herself with a gold blanket.

She left a note that said in part:

I am now about to make the great adventure.

Larry

Remember when you asked me
if I knew how to make coffee
when I emerged from the bedroom
before the sun was up that morning
after I'd driven 480 miles
to be with you when your wife
had died, and I found you
pacing outside the door
like an expectant father
who had panicked
when everything you'd
learned in childbirth
education class was gone
at the moment you needed
to be present, to be supportive,
to focus and to take care
of business and I said sure
I can do that, but you have
a coffee maker in the kitchen,
and you looked confused,
and we went out there
and sure enough there it was,
and I asked you where's
your coffee, and you didn't
know, and so I searched
the cabinets until I found
everything I needed
and while I was making
the coffee I noticed

the Post-it notes on the
counter and fridge
that your wife had left
reminding you to put out
the trash and to take your pills
and then you and I sat
at the table and drank
our morning coffee in a house
that seemed somehow empty.

Follow Your Bliss

for Joseph Campbell with thanks

Everyone in my high school
graduation class of 811 students
was given the Kuder Preference Test
to help us plan for the right careers
based on our specific needs.
It was said that the test assessed
our interests and suggested education
and career options. It was part
of the cradle-to-grave testing
industry that we all had to endure
even though some of us didn't
fulfill our destinies
and become acupuncturists
or funeral service managers
or elevator mechanics
or hot-dog cart vendors
as the Kuder people said
we should, we did the best
we could and now most of us
are retired and a good number
of us are in assisted living
and senior care facilities
where the Kuder people
have again found us
and somehow convinced
those in charge that we
need to take their latest
preference test which,

if administered correctly,
reveals what careers
we should have followed,
but didn't. The insurance
salesman is told he should have
become a dentist. The human
resource manager is told she
missed her calling
as a feng shui consultant
and the tired office manager
is told she should have been
a bike courier, which has led
to some tears and fits
of depression, but that's what
the pharmaceutical industry is for.

Skeletor Learned a Valuable Lesson This Week

It's not good to lie, cheat, and steal, unless you're a CEO in the fossil fuel industry engaged in a little bribery to help your bottom line or head honcho in a bloated telecommunications company, underreporting costs and inflating revenues with fake accounting entries or a high roller in the waste management business who just happens to report billions of dollars in bogus earnings to meet stockholder's expectations or an executive in a global financial services firm who hides billions in loans disguised as sales or maybe just a nice guy who loves his wife and kids and engages in a little bid-rigging and stock price manipulation in one of those multinational insurance corporations and so, remember boys and girls, no matter what a stranger says, never get in the car with him, unless he tells you how smart you are and how you're just the person to recognize a gold mine when you see it, and he offers you an opportunity to invest a few thousand dollars in the next big thing, so you can double or triple your money in less than six months. Then it's okay. And remember what Andrew Vachss said, *Business is a religion. Probably the only one practiced all over the world.*

Bye now.

On the Bookshelf at Night

Charlie Chaplin
as the Little Tramp
seated on a café chair,
leans over his cane
and stares down
at the floor,
thinking perhaps
of the lounging cat
bookends that keep
the old mystery novels
secure and in place.
The Big Sleep
and *The Long Goodbye*
aren't going anywhere,
and the healing drum
close by is at rest.
The only thing
that may concern
the famous clown
is the four-inch
Frankenstein monster
reaching out
from the shadows;
although, his gesture
seems to imply
that at this moment
he'd like to dance,
to shake off a bit
of cosmic dust.

There would be time
enough later
to be chased
by angry mobs
with pitchforks
and torches,
howling in the gloom
of superstition,
Kill the Monster!
And time enough
for a McCarthyite
"reds under the beds"
witch-hunt to hound
Charlie and chase him
out of the country,
but for now,
in the dark,
on the shelf at night
the two figures whirl
about with a graceful
unmerited divine
wind at their backs.

About the Author

Terry Allen is an emeritus professor of Theatre Arts at the University of Wisconsin-Eau Claire, where he taught acting, directing and playwriting. He is the author of the chapbook *Monsters in the Rain* and his full-length poetry collection *Art Work*. His poems have appeared in many journals, including *I-70 Review*, *Third Wednesday*, *Popshot Quarterly*, *Cloudbank*, *Into the Void* and *The Main Street Rag*. He lives in Columbia, Missouri with his wife Nancy and their dog Jayden.

www.ingramcontent.com/pod-product-compliance
Lightning Source LLC
Chambersburg PA
CBHW032011080426
42735CB00007B/572